Leading a Man to Clarity

By

Eric Smith Jr.

COPYRIGHT © 2022 BY ERIC SMITH JR.

Printed by:

Hancock Ghostwriters

Printed in the United States of America

First Printing Edition, 2022

ISBN 979-8-9861000-0-5

Dedication

For my grandfather John Henry Lewis. A beautiful spirit that ignited a fire within the depths of my soul.

Acknowledgment

I am extremely thankful for everyone who has ever said something of value to me because it has given me perspective and understanding.

All of my failed relationships and friendships have produced lessons that will remain with me and I am grateful for that.

Most importantly, I would like to thank God, for my strength comes from him.

Table of Contents

Chapter 1..1
Stop Comparing..................................1
Chapter 2..6
Live as if you know your Death Date............6
Chapter 3..10
Success Has Many Faces.......................10
Chapter 4..13
Always be Open to Criticism 13
Chapter 5..16
Adaptation..16
Chapter 6..18
Bird's Eye View 18

Chapter 7...*21*

Be Silent...*21*

Chapter 8...*24*

Character Building...*24*

Chapter 9...*27*

Empathy..*27*

Chapter 10...*29*

Unveiled..*29*

Chapter 11...*31*

Business First...*31*

Chapter 12...*33*

Importance of a Co-Pilot...............................*33*

Chapter 13...*36*

Enjoy the Movie..*36*

Chapter 14...*39*

Build Alliances *39*

Chapter 15...*41*

Be an Asset..*41*

Chapter 16..*43*

Validate Yourself..*43*

Chapter 17..*45*

Be a Sniper...*45*

Chapter 18..*47*

Stretch Out...*47*

Chapter 19..*49*

Blank Canvas...*49*

Chapter 20..*51*

Know Your WHY.....................................*51*

Chapter 21..*53*

Take Risks...*53*

Chapter 22..*55*

No Loitering...*55*

Chapter 23..*57*

Stand on Principle.....................................*57*

Chapter 24..59

Urgency...59

Chapter 25...61

Go Beyond Fear..61

Chapter 26...64

Out of Love 64

Chapter 27...66

Your Happiness is More Important............66

Chapter 28...68

Be the Security Guard of Your Life............68

Chapter 29...70

Real Pleasure...70

Chapter 30...72

Seasonal VS Permanent..............................72

Chapter 31...75

Power of Heart..75

Chapter 32...77

She Can Live in Emotion, You Cannot *77*

Chapter 33 .... *79*

Choose the Woman Wisely *79*

Chapter 34 .... *83*

Admire Your Woman *83*

Chapter 35 .... *85*

Match Her Energy *85*

Chapter 36 .... *88*

Lead Her Even When You are Unsure *88*

Chapter 37 .... *91*

Be Open to Loving Her *91*

Chapter 38 .... *93*

Your Purpose Comes First *93*

Chapter 39 .... *96*

Be Intentional with Her *96*

Chapter 40 .... *99*

Importance of Individuality in a Relationship..................99

Chapter 41.....................................102

Focus on Loving Her 102

Chapter 42.....................................105

Be Honest with Her 105

Chapter 43.....................................107

She Must Trust Every Part of You............107

Chapter 44.....................................110

Dealing with Pain................................110

Chapter 45.....................................114

Don't Blame Her 114

Chapter 46.....................................117

Grow Through It 117

Chapter 47.....................................120

Playoffs 120

Chapter 48.....................................122

Championship..122

A MAN'S PURPOSE

Chapter 1

Stop Comparing

Stop comparing your life to others and make your life the best it can be. People always want what they do not have, which is the biggest fight in our lives. When they say the grass is always greener on the other side, that quote is one of life's beautiful lies. We run after things that sparkle from afar most of the time, but when you look at them closely, you realize it was always an illusion you had.

In the modern-day, we have added to that pressure. We have access to many things. Due to globalization, the entire world is interconnected. What does that mean? It means that now we have access to the information we do not need. Platforms like Facebook, Instagram, and Twitter are all about glamorizing people's lives far from reality. But seldom do we realize that.

Because of that, men make the error of comparing their lives to others or people they observe on social media. It is only a way to deceive oneself. Most men will see someone of a similar age or caliber doing well in their lives which leaves them to ask themselves the most daunting questions "why do I not have what he has?" "Why haven't I become a millionaire?" "Why is he successful, and I still live at home with my mother?" As long as life continues, and you stay 100% invested in social media and compare your life to others, you will always feel inferior.

The modern world is designed where we are never satisfied with what we have. This is just another way for economies to flourish. "Create a sense of insecurity amongst people, so people buy more and more or try to be like others." For all the men, don't be fooled by the world that is run by the rich and elite. You are who you are, and the world needs your individuality and authenticity more than anything.

Life has become a show of unrealistic ideas. Everyday chores have become a source of insecurity, and men will often fall prey. This world is cruel to men; we already have enough on our shoulders. Too many expectations tend to weaken our minds and souls. When a man walks out of his home, he is swamped with illusions that make him feel less worthy. This can make a man doubt himself and wonder how other people are doing better than him. An illusion is just an illusion at best. It is a creation of your mind. An example for this is as simple as when you go to the grocery store or scroll through your social media; you always tend to find someone who is "doing better than yourself."

The keyword of the previous statement is "you." Nobody is better at being you than yourself. You are your only friend and savior, and no one wants a man in you who is NOT the real you. Comparing your life to others can be compared to running on an automatic treadmill. There is never really an end unless you press the stop button. You will keep running behind an illusion, and you are the only person who can stop running and get off that treadmill.

We have everyday examples when we are a slave to the world's riches. Most importantly, we are tied to our minds, allowing it to create an illusion for us, which is incorrect. A thing I tell all my male readers is never to follow what glitters for that will always come back to bite. A story that can help men achieve the right mindset is about a young man adamant about buying a new car. The father insisted his son purchase a Honda or Toyota due to his long daily commute. But, the young man did not budge and convinced his father he would buy a BMW, as one of his friends had bought one. The new BMW was flashed on social platforms, like Instagram, which ignited a sense of insecurity and desire in the young man who previously never cared about any car. The young man's father replied, "Son, BMWs are very nice cars, but the repair cost can be extremely high versus a repair of an economy vehicle." The young man disregarded his father and made it clear that he would be purchasing a BMW one way or another. The following day, the young man went to a local car dealership and purchased a 2006 525 BMW with 156,000 miles on the engine. The young man began posting the vehicle on social media, and his friends and family began celebrating with him. A few weeks passed, and the young man's check engine light turned on. Knowing that his friend had a BMW, the young man messaged him and asked him if he was aware of a mechanic who could assist. The friend responded, "Hey man, the BMW I posted on Instagram was a rental car; I would never purchase that thing." A bummer it must have been for the young man to realize that he was chasing an illusion. Did he need the BMW? Or was it an idea that seeped into his mind through social media that already glamorizes people's lives? We compare our lives to people when we don't know their stories or the truth behind their posts. People tend to share a picture-perfect life because this puts a soothing ointment on their insecurities and emotional injuries. People who post the "finer" things of life on social platforms are struggling through a myriad of problems. No one's life is perfect. How we define perfect can be different, though. Most people will never show you a sleepless night or a time when their stomachs ached due to hunger. Society only shows us highlights, leaving us feeling that we must hurry as if we are on a success time clock. YOU are the star of your movie; focus on the things that will improve your life and add to your purpose.

Chapter 2

Live as if you know your Death Date

Today, a common mistake is being made amongst men where opportunities are being missed. Many men are arrogant, believing they have a second shot at life. You only have one shot at life, and you must take your time, but take it seriously. If a letter was sent to your residence and enclosed was your death date, would it light a fire under you? Death is a whole subject. When so engulfed in the world we live in today, we often forget that life is temporary. Things are quick, and relationships are fleeting, money is brief. These are the most significant truths of life, but we chase these few things so that they fall off our radar. If we stop and think to ourselves that life is nothing but temporary, would we track all that glitter? Would we chase that BMW if we feel that there are other important things to accomplish in life?

Imagine a genie has appeared in your bedroom with the date and hour of your death. You would immediately google the most exciting things to do. You would think of your children and what you have left behind for them. You would go on YouTube and find ways to start a business or how to start a college fund for your child. You would feel as though you are on borrowed time. You would begin ignoring phone calls and removing friends that no longer serve a purpose in your life. You wouldn't cancel your gym membership to maintain your online porn or video game account. You would immediately prioritize your life and begin to handle business. You would save more money than you spend and remove the disrespectful woman you are with from your life. You wouldn't stay with her because you are afraid of leaving or are too comfortable in the relationship. You would immediately remember your value. Life is all about finding value in yourself instead of others, their journey is different from yours, and you have a different path to take. People's timelines do not match. For some, success comes quickly. But, if we are sucked into the fakeness this world has to offer us, then we are doomed. Value comes from realizing that you have it all. You have all the tools to be whomever you want to be, and you do not have to chase anyone.

If you knew when you were dying, you would focus your energies on things that would impact your life and after your life. You would begin reading books that would ignite ideas and educate you on important history you were unaware of. You would attack every single day this way. When you are tired and don't want to work out, that is the day you must go. When that voice in your head says, "just stay asleep," That is the time you should get up and go exercise. Everything you do in life is connected whether you believe it or not. For example, when you wake up in the morning and leave home without making your bed, there is a high chance your day will start rough. If you wake up, go for a run, and make up your bed, you will likely have a very productive day because you started it off with accomplishing something (working out and making up the bed). Attack life and lock in on the things you want. If you don't know what you want in life, remember that you know your death date, and the idea will come to you.

That is why it is better to live in the moment and look at your inner self. When we look outside for validation for our success, we will invariably become disappointed. This is because we consistently rate ourselves from a flawed perspective. We judge ourselves from the success scale of others. But we were all born different, and we will all be men who are beautifully unique in our ways. There is no definition of a perfect man. The ideal description for perfection does not even exist. So how did men start trying to achieve perfection when we do not even know what it is.

Chapter 3

Success Has Many Faces

As humans and men of this world, we come in different forms. We are divergent looking, we come from opposed backgrounds, and most of all, we all are destined for contrasting things. You will never see two people with the same success or failure stories. Similarly, our purpose and mission in life are all unconnected. We aspire to do unassociated things and have singular likes and dislikes. Somehow yet again, we compare ourselves to men walking an unrelated path from that of ours. Yet we never begin to stop and wonder why we measure our success from a man who has unique experiences.

We glorify things that others make us believe are special, not because they are unique. Men today seem to have lost the value of the saying "provider." Men will do illicit activities to provide or even go as far as committing a crime. The true purpose is to be a provider and a sustainer. Due to his irresponsible actions, a man cannot offer or sustain while in jail or deceased.

Today, society has told men that there are only three routes to success: athletics, entertainment, or illegal activity. Also, women have glorified these three categories, which makes an average man want to chase after them. They overlook their passions and want to do the next dope thing women want. Society has pressured men into becoming someone they are not and were never meant to be, only to uphold a certain standard. For men being the desired mate for women is paramount, which is why they succumb to the social standard. In the 1970s, it was not uncommon for men to do hard labor jobs six days a week. This required men to be the sole provider of households while the wife took care of the home. Ladies, I understand that you can hold the same positions as men; I am just getting to a point. These hard labor positions were construction workers, warehouse workers, plumbers, mechanics, and sanitation workers. These jobs were not frowned upon; they were respected positions. Society could not correctly operate without these positions being occupied by hard-working men. Today, these same positions are frowned upon and are not considered "sexy." You rarely hear or see people admiring a sanitation worker or construction worker. These men who occupy these positions can earn up to six figures and have the benefits to secure their families in a catastrophic event. These men can sustain families and provide. Men, you must understand that success will look different for each individual. Lebron James was destined to go to the NBA and be a superstar. Your destiny may be that you open up a million-dollar health insurance company. Whatever success is for you, just make sure it allows you to provide for your family and live comfortably. Don't allow societal pressure and toxic women to tell you what success looks like. The woman for you will not care what your profession is. The woman for you will just want you to do what makes you happy, puts you into the best position to be a provider, and do what has the highest probability of you making it home to your family. Remember, success is whatever you want it to be; just be a provider with whatever your chosen profession is.

Chapter 4
Always be Open to Criticism

To better yourself, you will always have to introspect. There are places within you that need development. Most of the time, men do not realize they need fixing. By fixing, I mean shifting their minds and developing a better perspective of life. By improving, I mean to open up to others to allow self-improvement. Men can be very rigid and often think they are lone wolves and can fend for themselves. The truth is we do not know ourselves honestly. Getting to know oneself is a lifelong journey that needs years to complete. One may ask, "what could make this journey more fluid and healthy?" Well, it is to hear and accept constructive criticism about yourself.

Men have an issue with accepting criticism or holding themselves accountable. Men are meant to be leaders in their communities, but you must be open to criticism and opinions of others because it could open your mind or challenge you to be better.

According to Webster's dictionary, criticism is defined as "the expression of disapproval of someone or something based on perceived faults or mistakes." Let's dive into this definition a bit. A person does not always need to be unhappy or upset with a particular topic about yourself. A person may believe you can improve in a specific situation or enhance a particular business idea. That is okay, and one should be open to such advice or criticism, whatever it may be. Sometimes people look at us and our situations from their own experiences, and we can never look at our position in the same light; hence it is always a good idea to listen to what people have to say. There is no need to follow what they say blindly, but as a wise man, you can always give some weightage to your friends or family's advice.

When I was a police officer in California, I spoke with a young man I will refer to as Joe. Joe was raised in the southern side of the city, which was known for being violent. Joe was an individual that would stand outside on the corner with other young men. I contacted Joe one day in

2020 and told him that it was a war in the city, and he was making himself an easy target. Joe responded with, "I am from this city; nobody will do anything to me." I told Joe to take care of himself and be safe, and I drove away. A few weeks later, I responded to a call of shots fired, and the reports stated that there were 16 shots heard. I arrived at the scene and saw a crowd of 8-10 young men surrounding an unknown object. I observed Joe lying on the ground with a single gunshot wound to his upper left chest as I walked closer. To the left of him, I saw a 7.62 expended casing. 7.62 ammunition is typically used for high-power firearms. I stood above Joe and immediately began talking to him and telling him to keep fighting. I immediately realized that Joe was deceased. All I could think about was my last conversation with Joe and wishing he would have taken my criticism and advice seriously. In life, criticism doesn't always come from people we know or people we are fond of. We can sometimes be so focused on the messenger that we disregard the message. When people feel the need to mentor or critique you, be humble and embrace the information that can assist you. Accepting criticism can be the difference between life and death, promotion and firing, and happiness and unhappiness. Be a sponge in life and absorb information.

Chapter 5

Adaptation

Men must understand that life is full of swift transitions. Things may be going exceptionally well, and they may fall apart in a blink of an eye. Always be prepared for the next thing and keep an open mind.

When I was 23 years old, my mentor and a long-time friend told me, "life is full of swift transitions." At the time, I did not truly understand the importance of this statement. As I progressed and made changes in my life, I realized that he reminded me to constantly adapt to any situation. As men, we sometimes get so comfortable at a job or even in a relationship that we stop doing the things that made us such a hot commodity in the first place. Sometimes, when these things happen, we are let go or fired. We feel worthless, sad, and even insecure when we are let go. Whenever things occur unexpectedly, I always hear my good friend's words, "life Is full of swift transitions." If you can always keep an open mind, you will always come out of any situation a winner. If we look at everything in life as impermanent, we will find delight in new things. Life sometimes makes us feel as if we possess things, but the truth is the only permanent part of life is death. Appreciate what you have while you have it, but understand each day may present the unknown. Adaptation is the key to life. Embrace the unknown with a fearless attitude and a heart filled with compassion, and you will always be able to adapt to any given situation.

One thing I have learned about life is that nothing comes easy. Men have to understand that they should lead a life as it comes and make decisions based on the context. The world is constantly evolving, and with technological changes, we can never be complacent; we need and will have to keep growing to keep up with the times and bring in some flexibility in ourselves.

Chapter 6

Bird's Eye View

Brothers, having a bird's eye on your life will ensure you stay focused on the essential things. Never get caught up in the "now" or a short-term failure. Keep your eyes on the entire painting, and I promise you will find beauty in it.

Men today need to understand that they must be leaders. True leaders keep a bird's eye view on situations because they know things are never as bad as they seem, and in the grand scheme of things, they might not even matter. For example, a man is fired from his job and has no other source of income. However, this man has a beautiful wife and children and has a roof over his head.

The majority of us would panic and become stressed out, thinking about how we will pay the bills. But why not view this situation as an opportunity to invest in yourself or to become a better father? I know we are taught to have tunnel vision in life and focus on ourselves, but if we keep a broad view of situations, we will always be optimistic regardless of the circumstance.

Let's get back to the example, so the man goes home and tells his wife that he has been fired. His wife replies, "honey, you have cared for our children and me for 20 years." She continued, "I want you to start that insurance company you've been speaking about."

See, his wife has a bird's eye view of things and understands the importance of gratitude. Gratitude and having a bird's eye view are the same. Having a bird's eye view of things means you recognize the good you have in your life and understand that sunshine will come after the rain.

As leaders of our families and in our community, men must always be optimistic and understand that pain is temporary. The strength of your family comes from your confidence. If your wife sees you stressed out and drinking to numb the pain, she will lose faith and trust in you, and things will tumble down the drain sooner than later. All of this can be avoided by simply understanding that looking at things from a higher view will give you a better perspective.

For example, a pilot can see if a runway is clear and its surroundings minutes before landing. Be the pilot of your life and slow things down. Never rush, and never fall into the temptation of things that can lead you to crash and burn. Always consider every outcome, and you will always be satisfied with the results, gentleman.

Chapter 7

Be Silent

You must keep people off balance and constantly guessing. It is not that telling people about your plans and success will jinx it. Being silent just creates a mysterious aura around you.

Men today must understand the power in silence. We have been taught by society that being the loudest gets you noticed. Well, being the loudest gets you seen, but it also allows people to figure you out. We live in a predatory society, where people are constantly searching for a flaw in you. Once the defect is identified, they will exploit that flaw and attack that area of weakness to their benefit.

Listening is an art. You must allow others to speak as you simply listen. You must master the ability to listen to others while giving little of yourself. We often make the mistake of telling short-term friends our life stories and even our deepest secrets. Sadly, when you and that friend have a disagreement and fall out of the loop, your information will no longer be sacred—confirming that basic decency is hard to find in others.

Keep your plans and goals to yourself. When you begin to express these things to people, you give them the opportunity to have an opinion about you and your life, and some will discourage you. In the movie Godfather, Don Corleone said to his son Sonny, "Never tell anyone outside the family what you are thinking." Mr. Corleone understood the importance of silence because when you cannot control your tongue, it gives a potential threat to a possible target.

You must keep people confused and off-balance by never revealing your true intentions. Leave people unprepared and guessing and allow them to create the story they believe is appropriate. But, you must never validate the story, nor should you ever respond in agreement or disagreement. You must work toward your goals and remain silent as you walk the path of success.

The more they assume who you are and what you are thinking, they will walk down a path of self-sabotage by making a defense against your next move that they are unsure of. By the time they realize your move, it will be too late, and they will be left wondering. Stay silent and listen more than you speak, brothers.

Chapter 8

Character Building

You must always work on your character and strive to make it better every day. Working on character does not require perfection, but just the will to succeed.

Men must realize that every obstacle creates character. The key is how one responds to obstacles and what his approach to life's adversity is. Every man will have moments in his life where he feels nothing is going right. He will devote himself to his woman and children, and she will still leave him. He will devote himself to an occupation, and he will be fired. He will give his last to loved ones, but they will not reciprocate his love. You must respond to these obstacles with fire in your heart and be present in the emotions drawn from each circumstance.

When you are present in each moment, you can receive the lessons with an open heart. However, in order to ensure that you are present in each moment of catastrophe, you should immediately take responsibility for the role you played in the incident. By holding yourself accountable, you can only grow from the situation.

It is easy to say, "my wife wasn't for me," or "my manager didn't like me." But, a man of good character will say, "I could have been a better communicator," or "I didn't work as hard as I should have." Men of good character don't lose in life because everything is a lesson.

My father is a famous musician who goes by "Pikfunk." One day when my father was a child, he told his father that he wanted to play the bass guitar. His father replied, "boy, you barely know how to play the drums; you can't play no bass." My father sadly walked away feeling discouraged from a man he admired.

The next day, my father made a decision that he would prove his father wrong. He took control of his situation, and not only did he become a world-renowned bass player, but he also became proficient on the drums. He worked relentlessly to become the best bass player he could and became a student of the game.

Before his father passed away, he religiously gloated about my father and his many successes. My father would go on to win a Grammy Award in his career and share the same stage with the likes of Janet Jackson and Rihanna. He accepted the challenge and looked at his father's words as an opportunity to learn a lesson. And that is what good character is based upon. It is built when you accept responsibility and hold yourself accountable for the outcome of any given situation.

Chapter 9

Empathy

Empathy is the ability to see through another person's eyes, the ability not to be standing in someone's shoes, but the willingness to put the shoes on your feet to allow them to feel that you are present, that you are there for them.

Today, it seems as though men have become very reactive to criticism and are quick to respond to negative comments made about them. This is not just plain immaturity but also an absolute waste of time and energy. You must quickly understand that people will only grasp a person or topic based on their understanding. It is simply a waste of time to attempt to persuade an individual to think the way that you think. You can go your entire life trying to prove yourself to a person, but the fact is that they can only comprehend a topic based on personal experiences.

When you are met with individuals at work or your gym who have a hard time understanding you, you should simply respond with empathy in your heart. You must say to yourself, "This person is only doing what they feel is right, based on their views of society."

We cannot control anything but our own views and principles. You must realize that even those who make poor decisions or those who judge people are only practicing the same right to view the world through their lenses. Regardless of how absurd or offensive that opinion might be, they are entitled to it. When you are met with negative criticism from people who see you as their competition, you must exercise empathy. You should feel sorry for a person who would waste valuable time and energy to discredit or invalidate the person you are.

You must also pay close attention to the character of the people who attempt to assassinate your reputation to remind yourself what you do not want to turn into. The person that has attempted to do this is basing their importance on invalidating you. How sad is it that someone must push someone else down to raise themselves up? You must empathize with people and hope that their lives can become better. You should never take offense to unadvised criticism but instead feel pity for the messenger as they are the ones at a loss, not you.

Chapter 10

Unveiled

All men are born into this world unclothed, and we should leave this earth unclothed.

There is no value in walking on earth while also playing it safe. Every day, you must ensure that you dominate the universe and leave your mark even if it costs a man his life. The moment a man accepts death and realizes it is inevitable, he becomes free, free from the bonds of society and tradition and whatever keeps him from living his life.

Many people will go their entire lives playing it safe to prevent death as if it is something that can be avoided. In 2020, a plague attacked the world and claimed many people's lives. In that group of people were adventurous people, military veterans (including my grandfather), first responders, and elementary school teachers. The group is very diverse, and ironically, they all met the same fate.

I learned from the plague to enjoy life and attack each day until your goals are accomplished and stay consistent till that happens. You should have given so much of yourself on earth that you can smile when you are on your death bed, knowing that your tank was empty. Imagine the feeling of knowing you gave your wife every part of you. Imagine the feeling of knowing you were an amazing father to your children. Imagine the feeling of knowing that business idea became a million-dollar business, and now you can take care of your family even after death.

You should want to leave this earth ultimately unveiled with nothing left to give to society and nothing left to take from it.

Chapter 11

Business First

Men must always put their purpose and responsibilities first; everything else is secondary.

In 2013, I was a student-athlete at Pittsburg State University, living in an apartment with my older brother, Graylon, who was also a student-athlete. One evening I was working on an assignment due the following day. I was attempting to work on the project, but I thought it was more important to talk on the phone.

Hours passed, and I still hadn't completed the assignment because I was distracted the whole time. My brother called me into his room, and he told me to have a seat on the edge of his bed. He said, "nothing is more important than your business, you handle business first, and only then you should allow yourself to do other things."

At that moment, things began to click for me. I realized that I was allowing outside factors to hinder my progress. I vowed always to take care of business before I played from that day forward. You may get invited to an event that you have wanted to go to for a year, but you have to get rest for your presentation at work. The unsuccessful person would go to the event and enjoy themselves but be unprepared for the exhibition. At the same time, the successful person will tell their friends to record the event for them due to them needing to be well-rested for their presentation. That is the difference between being mindful of your actions that may hinder your growth and being dumb.

When you work hard and keep business first, you always put yourself in a position to succeed. When you focus on doing the things you have to do in the present, you set yourself up to do the things you want to do in the future.

Chapter 12

Importance of a Co-Pilot

If a plane goes down and the pilot struggles, the co-pilot must take over and land the aircraft safely. That is the duty of a partner.

Over time, men have lost the value of having a good teammate in a woman. Men have only viewed women as objects that will compliment them in pictures and provide them with sexual pleasures. A woman's looks will fade, and a man's sex drive will eventually decline. However, a good partnership always remains.

My brother Naeem aka 'Dreebo,' attended Missouri S&T University and graduated with his Bachelor's Degree in Engineering. In California, it is estimated that engineers make approximately $100,000 yearly. Naeem was set for his future, and awaiting him was a high-paying job with great benefits. Soon, Naeem left Missouri, returned to San Francisco, CA, and started living with his wife.

He was a scholar-athlete, and everyone knew it, but Naeem had bigger plans. Naeem wanted to be like the legendary west-coast artist he used to admire while growing up in Los Angeles, California. He wanted to be a rapper. And he knew that people around him would say things like, "How typical," or "Why would you walk away from six figures in engineering?"

However, Naeem didn't care about the opinions of others but only focused on his craft. Naeem's wife was beautiful, a college graduate, and came from a very successful family. All of these qualities mentioned above are important in a woman.

However, her most important quality was her ability to be a good teammate and support Naeem. She didn't care about what her parents would think or how long it may take for her to reap the benefits of Naeem's music. She vowed to stay in his corner and support him like no other and even continued to work as he spent countless hours in the studio.

In 2020, Naeem opened up for Grammy Award Nominee' Schoolboy Q' in Oakland, CA. His wife stood and smiled as Naeem performed on stage, and he smiled back in admiration for the best teammate he could have asked for in this life.

Men, the woman you choose to marry or share a life with is one of the most important decisions of your life. If Naeem's wife had decided to discourage his dream or scold him, he would have lived a greatly unfulfilling life outside of his purpose. Don't just choose a woman for her looks or sex appeal. Choose the best teammate for all the difficult decisions and situations you may face.

Chapter 13

Enjoy the Movie

Stop trying to predict the next scene in your movie. Just have your popcorn ready and enjoy the ride. Life is as unpredictable as it gets, and spending your moments trying to decipher it will only add to your worries.

Have you ever gone to a movie and been with someone who constantly attempts to predict the next scene or outcome of the film? I believe we all have, and it became draining for the recipient of the questions and took away all its fun. Imagine the stress of a man attempting to predict or control the outcome of every situation in his life. You can never truly relax or enjoy life because you spend time thinking of every possibility. Instead of guessing the next scene of your life, focus on controlling the things you actually can control.

Let's take a look at some of the things you can control:

- Your attitude

- How you treat people

- Your happiness

Outside of all the controllable situations, we must not stress or worry. Worrying about things you cannot control is like staring at your hair, waiting for it to grow. You cannot control how fast your hair grows or when it will grow. However, you can focus on washing your hair and moisturizing your scalp to assist with the growth of your hair. You can control the products you put in your hair, but you still cannot control how slow or fast your hair will grow.

Instead, enjoy the process and take the lessons the hair growth process will produce. It is essential to be cautious of your decisions, but never forget that your mistakes develop character. Men must never put too much pressure on themselves to be perfect, but they must understand that they cannot be careless or completely reckless.

In the movie the Godfather, Don Corleone said to his son Michael Corleone, "I spent my life trying not to be careless; women and children can be careless, but not men."

Women and children follow the man's lead, the head of the family. If the family leader is careless, his family is at risk of falling apart and ultimately falling into the hands of ruins. You must understand that if you make a decision and it does not go as you wish, you can at least stand firm in knowing that you made the decision you believed was best and grow from it.

Chapter 14

Build Alliances

Building a robust community around you is the difference between successful and unsuccessful people. You are only as strong as your weakest link. Creating communication and networking is the key to success these days when the world is already a global village.

Whenever you see a successful man, you see a successful team behind him. Sometimes, these are childhood friends brought along, and sometimes these are people who feel indebted to this person. Whomever they may be, they have the commonality that they are in alliance with success.

Successful men understand that when you are of assistance to people and help them with their problems, you build many relationships. These relationships may not be able to reciprocate your gesture in the present fully, but they will strengthen the man of power and be of assistance to him in the long run. In this day and age, network quotient is of more excellent value than intelligent or emotional quotients combined.

Building solid alliances guarantee success because you are in the good graces of numerous people who will assist in any way that they can. The best business relationships are the ones that have been battle-tested and with whom you have built trust. A day will come when your finances may be low because life is unpredictable, and your alliances will have no issue loaning you money based on the time and trust developed through trials. Brothers, build strong partnerships, and it will bring the greatest return on your investment.

Chapter 15

Be an Asset

Make sure you always can bring something to the table. If you work in a barbershop and cannot cut hair, grab the broom and sweep up the hair. Being practical is the key to being in the loop of things.

If you are an entrepreneur or an employee, make sure you are always an asset. It would be best if you did the groundwork and constantly found ways to master whatever you are attempting to obtain. If you do not know how to do something, you must control what you are good at doing. For example, if you notice a leak in the building you are an employee at, place a bucket below the leak. You may not know how to correct the leak, but you have shown the willingness to find a temporary solution. That is when you become an asset and quite indisposable when you always bring something to the table.

On every team, everyone plays a role. Emmitt Smith is a hall of fame running back who had a phenomenal career with the Dallas Cowboys. Emmitt had God-given talent that was unmatched, but he would not have had the same job without his exceptional offensive line. Emmitt's offensive line was an asset to his career, and he understood the value in each individual. The offensive lineman could not run the ball as well as Emmitt, and he could not defeat the defensive lineman as they could. Everyone won't be the leader but can be a leader within their realm while simultaneously being an asset to the team.

Chapter 16

Validate Yourself

You will one day have an idea or invention that nobody finds meaningful besides you. YOU are all the validation that you need. Instead of seeking it from someone else, be proud of yourself first.

You will spend hours, nights, months working on an idea one day. You will present it to someone, and they will laugh and dismiss your opinion. Now, you might walk away and feel defeated because you thought that your idea was meaningful. You can leave this situation feeling defeated or let this situation drive you.

The problem is that we focus on the 400 dismissals but ignore the one approval. Sometimes the one approval is from self, from your own heart, and in the grand scheme of things, that is the only approval you need.

Legendary boxer, Floyd Mayweather Jr, lost in the 1988 Olympics to Sefarim Todorov. Mayweather could have allowed that moment to ruin his career and force him into early retirement before his time came. Instead, Mayweather realized that he had already claimed greatness and success over his life, and that was enough. Mayweather finished his professional career in 2017 and was 50-0. Mayweather validated himself and understood that he was significant even after losing as an amateur. He lived on to leave the sport of boxing regarded as the greatest boxer of the 21st century.

Sefarim Todorov ended his career in 2015 and was only 6-1. It is not about how you start. It is about how you finish. Life is a marathon, and at times, you will be exhausted and be far behind. The key is to validate yourself and believe in yourself. With this mentality, you will always succeed. The only approval you need is the man looking back at you in the mirror. If the approval of others is influencing you, you will be bound to fail.

Chapter 17

Be a Sniper

Be clear on your target in life and know exactly where you want to be. Knowing your plan ahead helps you out in more than one way.

Snipers in the military are expected to provide surveillance and reduce the opposition's combat ability. Snipers are expected to keep a long eye on high-value targets and monitor yards ahead to protect foot soldiers.

That said, accuracy and knowing what you are shooting at is critical. Most people go into situations blinded and unsure of what to expect. It would be to your benefit to focus on what you want in life with precision. This does not mean that obstacles won't come. You will be so focused on the goal that the barrier will not stop you.

It would be best to balance yourself, find your target, focus on your target, take a deep breath, then pull the trigger. Using that technique, I guarantee you will hit the bullseye.

To elaborate, being balanced means meditating, being clear on your intentions, staying fit, and eating healthy. Finding your target means you are learning the nuances of your target and ensuring that this target will place you where you want to be in your life; it is like making your way up the ladder, one step at a time.

Focusing on your target means that you are confident that this is your purpose in life. Now you must be relentless in mastering this target and be willing to progress daily to pursue this goal; it requires you to be consistent and unrelenting. Medical professionals say taking a deep breath in critical or stressful times enhances your mental clarity and brings you a sense of peace.

Now that you have completely locked in on your goal and are mentally clear, pull the trigger and watch the body of your goals succumb to your relentless pursuit. Hard work and persistence indeed get you through.

Chapter 18

Stretch Out

Like a slingshot, life's journey will pull you as far as possible, making you dance on your toes like a pendulum, to and fro, to and fro.

There will be a moment when you will be overwhelmed with your circumstances. You will be exhausted with work, tired of your boss, or frustrated with not accomplishing goals in your time frame. It would help a lot if you had the mentality of, 'this is what it is supposed to feel like.'

When you are heading toward your vision or goal, it is supposed to make you uncomfortable; it is like the fish trying to go against the current. In many ways, your goals or vision should feel like a burden. However, you must embrace this burden and smile with overwhelming confidence and prepare for the lessons the test will teach you.

Accept that you will be tired, but you must be a chameleon and adapt to all situations. Your pursuit of greatness will stress you out and sometimes leave you feeling that you may never reach the goal. There will also be times when you think your dreams have made you alone in the world.

These emotions and feelings are typical while in pursuit of your dreams. You must stick to the script, put it on your back, and carry the weight. When you feel low or want to give up, you must re-establish your goals when you are in the mind frame. Stretch out and push your limits because the world is limitless.

Chapter 19

Blank Canvas

It is better to create your painting regardless of the outcome. Whether it is a masterpiece or a failed attempt at art, it is always better to do it yourself.

You must always paint from a blank canvas and speak from your personal experiences. As you progress in life, you will see that the world will adapt to you as long as you stay true to yourself and do things in the way you can. When you are attempting to be someone other than yourself, you will draw in people or opportunities that only embrace the person you portray to be, and you will be setting yourself up for disappointment in the long run.

You may be given an opportunity, but deep inside, you will know that you can never indeed reveal the person you are to sustain this opportunity. You will become like everyone else and blend in. And this will eat you up from the inside because you won't be staying true to yourself.

Although the world will see you as successful and happy, you will have lost your individuality and authenticity. It's similar to comparing a cloned human being to an actual human being. The cloned human being will have all of the physical features of a human, but it won't be the same as a human-created in love by two humans.

Paint from a blank canvas and do things in the way only you can. There are things that only YOU can do because you are the only one of your kind.

Chapter 20

Know Your WHY

Men often allow life to happen to them and indulge in activities or an unfulfilling occupation because it is in trend or because it pays the bills.

Men must be sure of their 'why' or purpose in doing something. The most common belief amongst men who have a career is that they are working to live a happy life. These men often find that although they have everything they could ask for financially, they still lack true fulfillment.

Your driving factor cannot be self-fulfillment or living an exciting life. Your driving factor must be the service of others and happiness. With the assistance of others and satisfaction as your focus, financial profit will automatically derive from that.

This is the main reason why we often see millionaires committing suicide. From the outside perspective, they appear to have everything anyone can ask for, and anything money can buy, but the truth is they are unhappy.

When you gain a certain level of success, it becomes easy to lose yourself and your 'why.' It is easy to fall into a monotonous life pattern like a robot. If you always stay focused on your 'why,' only then will you be fulfilled. Even in the months when your business isn't bringing in money or your employer is being hard on you, you will remain fulfilled because you are focused on serving others.

Staying focused on serving others promotes humility because you understand everything is not about you and that the world doesn't revolve around you. The next time you feel sad or depressed, I challenge you to buy a homeless person lunch or help an older woman lift her groceries. You will immediately feel gratification because you know you served someone and made their day a little easier. Focus on service and watch positivity flow to you like a current in the ocean, enveloping you in blessings and glory.

Chapter 21

Take Risks

It would be best if you did the things in life that scare you or are uncertain for you to grow.

There is no value in playing it safe or blending in with the crowd. Thousands of men go to jobs they are unhappy at or stay in relationships they are unhappy with. We do this because of comfort and fear of change. We allow colleagues to convince us that we are lucky to have a particular job and not be ungrateful because many people would like to have what we have.

Remember, you are not being ungrateful for wanting better for yourself. People who are afraid and content with themselves will attempt to persuade you not to pursue greatness in your life. You will constantly meet people who discourage you from taking risks simply because they did not take risks themselves. When you are unsure of a career choice or personal relationship, ask yourself, "If I died today and my life was played back to me, would I feel satisfied."

If your answer is yes, continue to do the things you are doing. However, if your answer is no, you must immediately find the things that make you happy and fulfill you daily. If you leave a relationship you believe is no longer serving you and you soon realize you shouldn't have gone, at least you made a decision you thought was best for you.

As men, we must take chances whether the outcome is as we planned or not because this is how we grow and enhance our experiences. Experiences bring understanding and give us a reference point while operating through life. If your job is no longer serving you, make a plan and put yourself in a position to leave and do what makes you happy. It would help if you always remembered that taking a risk is one of life's most beautiful things. The beauty is found in understanding that you never lose when taking a risk because if it doesn't work, you can walk away knowing you made a decision as a man and did what YOU felt was right at the moment.

Chapter 22

No Loitering

You must constantly evolve and move forward. Life cannot be stagnant, and growth can only come out of constant change.

Have you ever seen a group of millionaires standing on the corner together smoking marijuana? Neither have I. According to websters dictionary, the word "Loitering" means to remain in an area for no apparent reason. You cannot say that you want success or be the best at your chosen profession by sitting still. You must constantly be active, whether that's in the physical or mental. People who loiter are often seen as lazy and unmotivated.

Never allow your mind to loiter and be focused on things that have no meaning because time is of the essence. Always make sure your mind is constantly working and locked in on things that will better yourself and the people around you. You are meant to be a leader and nothing less.

As the leader of your peers and your family, the attitude of everything depends upon you. If you are sluggard in your actions, your onlookers will be sluggard. If you are loitering physically and mentally, onlookers will linger too. If you are completely locked in on your goals and refuse to loiter in any area of your life, the team will follow suit. You will look back and see an unbreakable army behind you, following in your footsteps as you continue to lead from the front.

Chapter 23

Stand on Principle

Leaders focus more on standing on their belief system rather than the comfort of others because getting out of your comfort zone is what keeps you going.

Nowadays, it appears that our male leaders would instead comfort society than stand on principle. Standing on principle simply means to be firm in your beliefs or opinion on a specific topic and unwavering regardless of what you may be up against. You must be willing to lose everything to protect your principles rather than lose yourself in the process of saving others' feelings.

However, you must ensure that your principles are not fueled by negativity or immoral things. If your principles are built on the service of others and what you believe to be correct, stick to it and be willing to die for it. Imagine knowing that you went along with something only to further your career or get you that signing bonus you've worked so hard for. Yes, you've advanced your life, but you've lost a piece of yourself in the process.

In the Holy Bible, Mark 8:36 says, "For what does it profit a man to gain the whole world and forfeit his soul?"

You must be willing to be at war with the world but at peace with yourself. You will one day be in a powerful position where you will feel that many people are looking to you for an answer. You will be confronted with a challenging topic or situation that you know will ruffle some feathers if answered incorrectly. You must present a respectful response and a fearless response that is solely based upon what you believe in personally and what you know will be best for the masses, even if it is an unpopular opinion.

If you are scolded for speaking your truth, you will be able to sleep at night knowing that you did not lose your soul and stood on principle because resistance means you are doing something right.

Chapter 24

Urgency

Attack each day with a sense of urgency because you never know when it is all over. Live it as if it is your last.

We must wake up each morning with a sense of being and purpose. There are 333,638,357 people in the United States of America. A large number of the population are chasing success or the 'American Dream'. What separates you? Your hunger and commitment to your identified purpose will separate you and set you apart from the crowd.

It would be best if you were intentional in your actions. Stop doing things that don't serve you. That can be compared to putting gas into an electric vehicle. It will damage the vehicle and only cause you more issues. Treat life like a 24-second shot clock. You must take your time and find the best shot, but never lose track of time. Nowadays, Millennials are dying at an extremely high rate and have a short life span.

Live each day with a purpose, and always have your family in mind. Work to leave something behind for your family when your time on earth concludes. Many people will have lavish lifestyles and exotic cars but don't have life insurance. True leaders enjoy life, but not before ensuring that their family will be able to survive after they depart from this earthly abode. Be urgent in your life and get things done. Make a vow to yourself right now that you will no longer take life for granted.

Chapter 25

Go Beyond Fear

Fear is what separates you from success. It gets in your way.

Every man must dance in the spirit of fear and use it to his advantage when meeting opposition. You should constantly challenge yourself and face your fears head-on. Be mindful of the constant dangers you may face day in and day out, but be hungry in your journey.

Fear is the number one dream killer. Fear is your body warning you of something dangerous or destructive ahead. However, you should find peace in knowing that your body warns you and prepares you for the unknown. A man must be aware of his limits because the feeling of fear is also a security blanket to keep you from doing it. You must be able to relax in your sense of fear and still be highly productive.

Fear immediately reveals yourself and is the true image of who you are. Look at fear like the friend who always attempts to get you to go on a blind date, but you always decline. You should go on a date and face your discomfort. Get out of that comfort zone. You will find that the person you've gone on a date with is amazing and all you've been wanting, or you will find that this wasn't such a good idea. Either way, you've grown and faced a fear. You will be able to look at the situation with a broad scope and become more courageous the next time.

Being afraid of fear will force you to sit back, stay comfortable, and potentially miss a life-changing opportunity. Instead, fully embrace the opportunity and smile at your fear. When you smile at fear, it creates a sense of humanity and links you in arms with the many great men and women who have crossed the line of fear with passion.

For example, it is believed that Harriet Tubman led 300 enslaved men and women into freedom over ten years. Tubman had a $40,000 bounty on her head based upon freeing slaves during this time. Tubman was well aware of the consequences if captured, but she went beyond her fear and was spontaneous in her actions. Go beyond fear, and you will see a beautiful part of the universe you never knew existed because you refused to allow fear to get in your way.

Chapter 26

Out of Love

You should always do things out of love, even if the gesture isn't reciprocated. Love doesn't always have to be returned in order to grow.

Men must always do the right thing regardless of the outcome. Too many of us are conditional lovers meaning that we will love someone as long as the conditions are in our favor. True love is unconditional and will always promote sincerity within your heart. You must always do things out of love, whether the gesture is returned to you or not. It isn't your job to intentionally mistreat someone based on them not reciprocating your love.

You must remain in the masculine frame and control the things you can control. For example, if you are married to a woman and ask her to cook for you on Monday, and she refuses, you should not intentionally only cook for yourself on Tuesday. When you act out of emotion, your woman cannot fully love you or respect you.

You must focus on doing everything out of love and for the best interest of yourself first and the relationship second. If she is not receptive to your love and you begin to feel that you are giving more than receiving, it is time to walk away without waiting another second. The most powerful thing a man can do is walk away because it is you putting yourself first. When you walk away, you show the other party how much you value yourself, and you can stand firm in your masculinity, knowing the power you now hold.

Chapter 27

Your Happiness is More Important

It would help if you mastered the ability to put yourself first in relationships while still serving the other person. It is not selfish or self-serving, rather self-fulfilling.

Men, you must understand, the only way a relationship with a woman can last is if she believes that you are better than her or more superior. A woman must know that you are in control of your own life, and if she wants to be a part of your life, she will naturally fall under that control.

As a man, you should never bring a woman into your life and compromise for her comfort. If she looks at you like something that can benefit her and enhance her life, she will have to understand that she will be following your directive while she is with you. If she is resistant to your expectations, you should remind her that she follows the rules when she goes to her corporate assignment. She may complain about the workplace regulations, but she will still go into the workplace and do what she is told.

However, she will want to come into your life (which is your workplace) and force you to settle. A woman must earn her place in your business. She will expect you to bargain and place her as the head manager, but you must let it be openly known that she will be starting as the janitor of your establishment. People cannot just come into your life without proving their value. Men must understand that they cannot just be financial and spiritual leaders; they must lead in merriment.

If you are miserable and depressed, your woman will follow suit. If you are cheerful and joyous, your woman will follow suit. You must lead from the front and ensure your woman knows that you are the star of your own movie. You must be comfortable in your masculinity and manhood and ensure you never degrade her in order to uplift yourself. You must be a leader in all ways for your woman to see you like royalty. Your woman must hold you in such high regard that she battles herself and her inner demons to ensure that she is only your peace and nothing and no one else's.

Chapter 28

Be the Security Guard of Your Life

You must ensure that you are keeping a close eye on who you allow in your world. Not everyone deserves to be in your world or in your life around people that you love.

Brothers, you must ensure you are securing the door of your life. You cannot allow just anyone to walk into your life. Like soiled boots ruin the carpets, some people will try to do the same with your life if you let them inside. You must be able to separate the difference between having a conversation with someone and allowing them into your bubble. You have to realize that when you allow just anyone into your life, you are also allowing them to bring their energy and opinions to you.

You need to study the people you allow to be around you seriously. Ensure that the people who want to be in your life show and represent who you truly are. If they are not showing you why they should be allowed inside, you must close that door. We live in a very toxic society where individuals will be portrayed as someone good for you but will only come to destroy everything you have built.

There is power in being isolated and being selective. These traits force people to wonder about you and your progress in life. However, a person who is meant to be in your life wouldn't have to wonder about you because they will have never left your side. If you do decide to reopen a closed door, you must wait until you are in a state of unattachment and are solid from head to toe. This person will return as everything you have ever needed in an attempt to play with your emotions. You must recognize the effort to trick you, close the door and place a deadbolt on it.

Furthermore, always keep in mind that the more you allow a person who hurt you to return, they are only viewing you as weak and dependent. The world depends on you and your leadership. You must rely on your logic and a clear conscience and be stern in your rejection of individuals who come to destroy you.

Chapter 29

Real Pleasure

True pleasure is found in fulfilling the desires of your heart. Of course, not all desires can be equally met, but something about giving your heart what it wants gives you immense pleasure.

Throughout history, we have been told that pleasure can only be sexual. Men today focus on status and being admired by women rather than pursuing solidity and happiness.

True pleasure was never meant to come from a woman. True satisfaction comes from manifesting an idea or invention and watching it come to fruition. You cannot call yourself a man if you are not productive. If you are not living in your purpose or working towards it, you are being unproductive.

A man that does nothing deserves nothing. You can't be a man that sits at home all day playing video games, but expect your woman to walk in the house and prepare you a meal. Those gestures are earned and not given. The same way a woman must work to be in your life, you must be walking in your purpose and masculinity every day so that the crown on your head can be seen from afar.

If you allow yourself to be unproductive, you will see your woman begin to disrespect you. You will ask her to rub your back, and she will laugh and say, "You haven't done anything all day; go to a massage therapist." See, this will occur if you focus on sexual pleasures and women rather than your purpose. You may have amazing sex with a woman, which will suffice for a short time, but eventually, the sexual pleasure becomes old. You can only truly stimulate a woman by advancing your life and living in your purpose. She must understand that nothing comes before your purpose and priorities. The more she understands that you are a man of meaning and dignity, you will see her submit in more ways than you could ever imagine.

Chapter 30

Seasonal VS Permanent

You must be able to separate between temporary people and permanent relationships. Not everyone comes into your life to stay forever; those who do are rare gems.

When choosing a companion or a friend, you must decide the time of the relationship. If you are around an individual and have an uneasy feeling, you must trust your intuition and understand that it may be time to allow the relationship to fade away. The problem when letting a seasonal relationship prolong is that the issues that may arise may become irreversible.

For example, imagine a man getting a woman pregnant who has bad intentions or a bad heart. He will suffer for the remainder of his life because he didn't pay attention to the relationship time clock. The universe will provide you with clear signs that the relationship is over.

Despite all of this, a permanent relationship will feel everlasting and bring you tranquility. The universe will begin to allow the person to suddenly bring up ideas to you that you never verbalized. The universe will have the person gifting you with items you have always wanted but never mentioned. It is very easy to get the two relationships confused because they both come in a similar fashion, a similar pattern. The only difference is only one of the two will be able to be consistent.

The irony is that the temporary relationship tends to appear as your perfect person, and the permanent person appears as a work in progress. Another way to tell the difference is to have the person complete an unorthodox task. The permanent individual will find a way to complete the task, while the temporary person will immediately tell you they will not complete the job or will come up with excuses to avoid it.

Being selective and paying attention to detail is an essential characteristic of a man, so you must be attention-oriented. By paying attention to the qualities of a person and not the surface, you will always quickly identify the one who is willing to stay around until the end of time.

Chapter 31

Power of Heart

When you work to have a heart in society, you will always remain at peace. Politeness and kindness are virtues very few possess, but it is always worth having the trouble or going the extra mile because the peace it brings you is unparalleled.

Nowadays, it seems that being polite to people and having a sincere heart is dying. You must actively work on keeping a positive outlook and being a king. Although we are in a predatory society, staying in tune with your heart is important. Growing up, we were all told the phrase, "Treat people the way you want to be treated." As young children, that was something we didn't like to hear. However, the saying is very clear. Why would you mistreat someone or speak negatively when that isn't the way you would like to be treated?

As a man, you must speak seldom, but make sure it is meaningful when you do speak. We are in a society where men will do anything to be noticed or seen versus doing what is right. For example, rapper Lil Nas X pretended to be pregnant in order to gain notoriety for his upcoming album. Had he been more mindful of his presentation, he would see the clear disregard for the pain women endure during pregnancy. Health professionals have said that a woman giving birth is relative to death for a woman.

As men, we must constantly be mindful of our messages to society. If we are loose-lipped, we will never be taken seriously, even if the message prepared is authentic. You will never go wrong when you focus on having a strong mind and a good heart. The problem comes into play when you begin to take actions that you know deep down are unethical, but you do them to appease others. When you keep hold of your heart, you will walk the earth with a light so bright that your peers will need sunglasses just to be in your presence.

UNDERSTANDING WOMEN

Chapter 32

She Can Live in Emotion, You Cannot

You must be able to use logic when dealing with women. They get the benefit of the doubt, but men cannot react impulsively. We must never lose the sense of logic.

Your woman may walk in the front door and immediately begin yelling about your tennis shoes she asked you to pick up that are sitting on the stairs. You will look at her and become confused, seeing how you have not seen her all day and haven't done much to provoke this response. You will respond with "honey, they are just shoes." She responds with anger and runs upstairs and slams the door.

Brothers, you must understand she is not upset about the shoes, but that is just the first thing she saw when she walked through the door. The issue may be that she has repeatedly asked you to show more affection on a daily basis, and you have refused to meet that need. You and your woman may be in an argument, and she may scream, "I hate you," and you will respond in anger typically.

However, you must understand that the feminine essence lives in emotion, and they change daily. Instead of responding with anger or confusion, run up to her, give her the biggest hug and ask her to relax and tell you of her concerns. Your woman must feel your masculine energy 100% of the time. If she thinks that you are as emotional as she is, she will lose faith in your presence, and your energy will be swapped with each other, and she will become masculine as you are on a downward spiral of emotional fragility.

Chapter 33

Choose the Woman Wisely

The woman you choose to date or marry will be one of the most important decisions you will make in your life. It will set your future in motion, and just this one decision can make or break it for your future generations.

Today, men have lost the true meaning of being a man. With the impact of social media, there is a shortage of leaders and 'real' men. Society has told us that 'assets' classify us. Well, women are classified by these assets as well. For example, a man goes to a club with his friends, and in his mind, he already has the type of woman he is looking for. So the man goes into the club, and he spots a beautiful woman (whom I will refer to as Brenda) who is easy on the eye with a surgically altered body. Standing next to that woman (who I will refer to as Chelsea) is a pretty woman, but she is not a head-turner.

Chelsea does not have an athletic body. In fact, she could use a trainer. The man begins walking toward the two women, and as he approaches, Chelsea grabs his arm. She says, "How are you?" And he pulls his arm away and says, "I'm not interested." So he approaches Brenda, whom he has had his eye on all night, and he refuses to leave without her phone number. He introduces himself, and they exchange information. As they are getting comfortable, his friend approaches and begins chatting with Chelsea. So, after they exchange information, she goes onto his Instagram account and see's his foreign cars and large home. Her eyes light up, and she says, "you taking me home with you tonight, right?" He smiles and nods his head, "Yes."

One year later, he and his friend go out for dinner to catch up since they hadn't seen each other since the club one year prior. He tells his friend, "Man, Brenda had a baby and now has placed me on child support." He continued, "She even called the police and told them that I hit her." His friend replied, "I am sorry to hear that, man, I ended up getting serious with Chelsea and proposing to her, and we started a real estate company." He continued, "She wasn't in the best shape when I met her, but now we go to the gym together."

Men, the woman that looks good for you may not be suitable for you. The exterior can always be adjusted with hard work, but a person's character and morals cannot be changed. Don't be a victim of lust and use the wrong head when picking the right woman. The gentleman in this story above was presented with two women, but one was not appealing to him. Had he given her the time of day or even been polite, he would have been able to gauge her character.

We become so focused on finding a woman who will get us compliments from our peers, or a trophy wife, that we forget to find a woman who will complement our lives. A woman is either giving to you or taking away from you. Leadership is the central quality women look for in a man, but we cannot be that if we are falling into lust. Had the man in the story been a leader, he would have seen the sparkle in her eye when she saw his assets, while Chelsea saw his friend as an asset.

Brothers, you must always stand firm on principle and stay in your masculine frame. Brenda knew that he was not in his masculine frame regardless of income. If you stay in your masculine edge, the woman that is not for you will immediately reveal herself, and you can dominate the world knowing you will not fall into temptation.

Chapter 34

Admire Your Woman

Your woman can only grow in love the more you show your admiration for her. It is the female psyche; it thrives on compliments and attention.

Growing up playing football, my coaches would get the most of me by challenging me or by putting me against another player. It can be challenging to break out these habits of using aggression when challenging people. However, when dealing with your woman, you cannot challenge her, instead express your love for her and expound on why you admire every part of her body.

If your woman has been gaining weight and has decided to put on a very revealing dress, you should tell her that she is beautiful but that you would rather you guys wear more casual clothing. See, you have made your woman secure in her beauty, but you have also accomplished your goal of removing her from a dress she can no longer fit.

Admiring women can be challenging for men because we have been taught to withhold our emotions, and truthfully many men have never been given a compliment by someone they love. It is something you must work at, gentleman. Even if you have to set a reminder on your phone to compliment your woman, do it. As time passes, it will become natural to praise and admire your woman; it will become your second nature.

You must find it in your heart to constantly remind her of how sexy she is as well. For example, we are in a society where natural women are degraded, and surgery is admired. That may mentally frustrate your woman or make her insecure. Your job is to remind her of her beauty and uplift her by reassuring her of your affection. Admiration will motivate your woman and unlock a part of her only a king will find.

Chapter 35

Match Her Energy

Don't run from it when your woman shows signs of fluctuating emotions. Instead, look for ways to gauge and better deal with her mood swings.

It is very challenging to deal with a woman's emotions because day in and day out, they change. I compare the changing of emotions to changing a baby's diaper (which should be changed every 2 or 3 hours). Women's emotions can sometimes feel like a burden to a man to the point that they overwhelm us, and we will often respond with, "I am going to the gym and will return when you are no longer annoying me."

This just makes your woman feel alone and as if you don't care about how she feels. You will never truly understand women or master them. Instead of trying to understand her, love her with a passion so deep that she can feel it pouring through your body.

The way you respond to your woman is the same way you will react to life's challenges. If your woman begins to scream at you and you decide to move out, you will quit your job when your boss moves you to another sector of the business. If you would rather gossip to your friends about your woman rather than stand up as a man and love her, you will do the same when you are short on your monthly bills. Instead of finding a solution for your woman, you will find excuses. A real man will take his hand off the steering wheel and understand that he can only control his response to any given situation instead of being proactive.

When your woman is emotional, you must stand tall in your masculinity and love her so strongly that she immediately forgets the reason she was upset and pours that love back into you. You must learn never to quit when challenges arise. You must dissect the problem and return to living with a whole heart. You must live your entire life with your heart full.

Don't treat your woman as some isolated item in your life, but rather as a meaningful gift that needs loving and reassurances. So, when she begins these rants and loses her cool, poke your chest out, grab her, give her the biggest kiss and tell her things will get better. You must look at her inconsistencies as a true reflection of society because life will be going great one day, and disaster will come next. Embrace the uniqueness of a woman and be grateful for the lessons they produce.

Chapter 36

Lead Her Even When You are Unsure

A time will come when you are unsure of which way to go; just make a decision and see how things unfold. Either way, you will come out of it grown and wiser.

We have all been taught to allow your woman to make her own clothing decisions or which makeup to wear. Your woman will ask you for advice on which shoes she should wear to her business meeting, and you will say, "I don't care, do whatever you would like." To you, this seems like no issue and as though you are giving her freedom. It is another instance of you being unable to make a decision or lead her. Making decisions is the best way a man can show his dominance within a relationship.

You must understand that a woman will make choices based on her feelings, but a man must make decisions based on the entire frame. Your woman will buy a $5,000 purse while knowing her car payment and mortgage are due. As a man, you must tell her to put the purse down and advise that you will purchase her the bag during December when the prices are lower. She may resent you at that moment, but she will trust you deeply.

For example, she may be considering quitting her job, opening up her own business, and asking for your input. Rather than being vague and replying in a general fashion, think deeply about her potential and say, "honey, I want you to be happy and follow your heart." You will continue with, "I want you to quit your job and follow your passion; I will ensure we are in good standing financially."

Deep down, you are thinking about the trouble of being the sole provider. However, to your woman, you have made the decision you believed was best, and this will challenge you to work harder as a man. If you have made the wrong decision or have given the wrong advice as a man, you can at least stand firm in knowing you made the decision you believed was best. As long as a man makes a decision and doesn't depend on the feminine emotion to do it and take over, he can always grow in his masculine essence.

Always guide your woman and assist her with tough choices, but also constantly remind her that she has your full support regardless of the outcome of her decisions. With that being said, make good practice of making decisions and explaining to her your thought process, and she will always trust you as her man.

Chapter 37

Be Open to Loving Her

Open your heart even when you are afraid; just be wise. You shouldn't give the impression that you are internally scared. You must conceal your fears for the better.

You must use your past relationships and experiences as a point of reference, but never let them hinder you or your growth. We all had that high school crush or first love that changed our outlook on relationships. You were sincere in your actions and truly admired her, and she left you for the 18-year-old who just graduated. This devastated you, and you closed off your heart. You began to sleep with different women to mask the pain.

As you grew into adulthood, you opened your heart again, had a similar experience, and are now closed off. However, as a man, you must always think logically and long term.

You must not stay in a place of anger or hate when dealing with women because you may push away the woman who will treat you like the king that you are.

Whenever someone you are dating doesn't appreciate you, always remember that a person not seeing your worth doesn't decrease your value. The truth is, they do not understand you. You must not take your past trauma out on a new woman because you may be doing to her what you did not want to be done to you in the first place. Remember that people can only see things from their view or perspective. No matter how much a giraffe attempts to convince a turtle about his life, the turtle will never understand simply because it is not on the same level.

You must keep these things in mind and understand that you must put your past trauma and mishaps behind you. Accept your role in the situation and move forward. After you have taken these steps and are ready to love fully, embrace your woman and love her in the best way possible without restraint. If it doesn't work, you gain understanding and knowledge and can walk away knowing that you followed your heart unapologetically.

Chapter 38

Your Purpose Comes First

A woman must always take a back seat to your purpose. She will soon walk away if she sees you will place her above all.

There will be a time when you are met with the decision of staying home with your woman or going to complete your work project. Your manhood below your waist will tell you to stay and make love to your woman. Your brain will remind you of the importance of this work project. You may think that if you stay with your woman, you are showing your dedication to her, and she will act as if she feels the same. You decide to leave and complete your work project, and she looks at you in defeat. You kiss her on the cheek, saying, "I will see you later." As you walk out of the door, she becomes upset and emotional.

Although she is upset that you have left, deep down, she understands that she is in a relationship with a purpose-driven man, and that thought makes her feel secure. In fact, you have blatantly proven to her that you are willing to sacrifice your time with her for your purpose. You must understand that intimacy is atop the list of women's priorities, not yours. Your priority is your purpose and focusing on the best route to achieve that purpose.

Alternatively, if you opt to stay in bed with her, she will appear outwardly satisfied. Consequently, deep down, she loses trust in you and will eventually walk away from you. Your woman must hate the moments you leave her, but understand this is necessary while pursuing your purpose. As much as society has attempted to convince us that women want to be a priority in our lives, they do not. If your woman becomes number one in your life, you must immediately isolate yourself and get back to understanding your purpose on earth. You must always strive to follow your mind and not your heart because a man must think logically instead of emotionally.

It is effortless to lose yourself in everyday activities such as the gym, playing video games, or sex. None of these will allow you to grow in your purpose. You must not sacrifice your purpose for temporary tasks. Your personal relationships don't need to suffer, but you must prioritize purpose above all. You can only be a high-level husband and father when you are living in your purpose. Your passion and commitment to your meaning will be present in all that you surround yourself with.

If you are not purpose-driven, it will be displayed in your actions, and eventually, your woman will oppose everything that you say. You will begin to feel that you are only seen as a man of the home because of your genetic makeup; nothing else holds you up to the standard. Gentlemen, your woman will appear as though she wants to be the focal point of your life, but she would much rather you be walking the earth in dominance while fulfilling your purpose. If your woman views you as someone who is purpose-driven, then she will have no problem following your directive.

Chapter 39

Be Intentional with Her

You must ensure you are doing everything with a purpose. There must be a goal associated with all that you do, a far-sighted vision to steer your boat and keep it steady.

Make a habit of being intentional in every area of your life, especially with whom you intend to spend a life. Many of us will see a woman's physical beauty and say the right things to get her into bed. We get her in bed and have an unforgettable sexual experience, but you somehow feel bad about yourself. You don't even realize that sex with someone is a transfer of energy.

For example, when a man ejaculates after sex, he becomes weak and most likely will fall asleep. The majority of the time, a man will ejaculate during sex, but the same cannot be said for women. So here you lay numb and lifeless as she is wide awake on her cell phone telling her friends about her horrible sex experience with you.

Rather than rushing her into bed, take your time, get to know her, explore her mind, seek her intellect. You must be more interested in making her mind climax before her body. When you focus on the mind of the woman, you can genuinely identify if the woman is actually for you. If you focus on the exterior, you will miss out on certain factors pertaining to her.

For example, you meet a woman, and she expresses to you that 'men are no good' or 'men are only good for sex.' If you are only focused on her exterior, you will be hurt by her words and run away from her. An intentional man will take a deeper dive into her mind and inquire why she feels this way. She responds and says, "growing up, my father was never around, and I just never saw the value in a man." The intentional man will show this woman empathy, remind her of her beauty, and show her that he is nothing like her father.

Let her know that you cannot remove the pain of her father being absent but that you can love her through her pain. You must intentionally be persistent and even advocate for her to speak with her father about his shortcomings. In doing this, you have given her a pathway to closure and have shown her the leader and comforter she has always yearned for.

You will be reminding the little girl inside of her that she can let go and trust you with her heart. She will trust you in a way that she never knew she could trust a man. When you are intentional, you can discern in relation to this woman and decide if the battles she is fighting can be repaired by your intentional love. Only an intentional man can be of assistance to a broken woman because only he is paying close enough attention to her.

Chapter 40

Importance of Individuality in a Relationship

Your individuality is the reason she loves you. No one likes mediocrity, especially women, who try as hard as possible to be different.

People in relationships have the misconception that they are supposed to do everything exactly the same as their partner. I understand that wearing matching onesies during the holidays is cute, but I am referring to things such as going to the same fitness center and church. You must understand that time away from your woman is key. That is where you keep your mystique and are able to grow as an individual to, in turn, be better for her.

The problem is that we are now in a culture where being obsessed with your partner and hanging over their heads all the time is considered love. Love is understanding that your partner had a life before you came into it and should be able to continue to do the things that made themselves happy.

However, if she is doing things that are disrespectful to you and your expectations, you must advise her that you are not pleased. If she does not correct the error, remove yourself from the relationship. If she is simply going shopping or going to the nail shop, don't bother her for the time she is gone and give her the freedom and room to miss you.

Men, you must understand that she was interested in you because she saw that you were not entirely focused on the pleasure of women. She saw that you were focused on yourself and working on your mental and physical health. The problem is that we get into these relationships, stop working on ourselves and our personal growth, and invest everything in the other person.

You must constantly be doing things to better yourself and spending the much-needed time away from her. When you are away from her, do things that can better your life and bring you a sense of peace. For example, when I am having a stressful day, I read books and work out. Both of those activities will enhance me as a man and, in turn, make me more attractive to my woman.

Despite this, men will leave home after an argument with their woman and go smoke marijuana or drink alcohol to numb the pain. You have only pushed the issue to the back of your mind, but you will sober up, and the issues will arise once again like bubbled-up yeast. If you have not found a positive outlet for negativity, you must find it. Hold to your individuality if you want to keep the relationship fresh and fun. The moment you make her the highlight of your life and the only something you are interested in, she will leave you. Take pride in having your own identity, for it can only bring out the best of you and your lover.

Chapter 41

Focus on Loving Her

Focus on loving her and growing in love rather than the outside world. The world can wait and will be the same every day even if you pay no attention to it. However, paying attention to your woman means letting her know that you acknowledge her importance in your life.

We must return to the time when loving her was more important than posting your love for her. We will post our women and gain public gratification but will lose the connection. You must ensure you have built a strong foundation that can handle the pressure of being 'Instagram official.' You must not be so concerned with proving to your peers of how happy you are. You must be more focused on ensuring that she has five positive attributes per each negative attribute.

For example, if she cannot cook, she must respect you, be encouraging, caring, treasures teamwork, and will bring out the best in you. Be certain that the woman you are posting possesses these attributes. We will post a woman because we know she is easy on the eye and will result in a large number of likes on an Instagram post.

The problem is that many of us will also post a woman based on believing that is the right way to do things or to please her when it is the exact opposite sometimes. You must pull from the positive relationships you have seen throughout your life. Don't allow social media to define what love should look like.

For example, my mother and father have been married for 28 years. My father is a traveling musician and spent a lot of time out of the country providing for his family, leaving my mother and me alone. I can recall on multiple occasions my father being in another time zone and calling me, reminding me to look out for the flowers he sent home for my mother.

This was a regular action from my father, and this showed me how to love a woman. My father taught me at a young age the value of a strong woman and going the extra mile to see her smile even when you can't physically be there. My father may have posted my mother a handful of times during this social media era, but my mother and father have never separated. My parents focused on respect and love, not reminding the world of their status. The world does not need to know everything about your life.

Refrain from posting your relationship too quickly. Instead, grow in intimacy with her, or you will view your relationship based on the world's perception rather than reality. For example, you don't plant a tree and invite friends to come to see the tree before it has developed. Allow your relationship with her to develop and become healthy and battle-tested. Even when they begin to speak negatively, you can withstand the storm. Put an end to telling the world about your woman and how special she is. Instead, remind her and love her unconditionally and become an unbreakable team that can take the world any given day.

Chapter 42

Be Honest with Her

Honesty is something that can be tough and not always pleasurable. Either way, tell the truth, and you will be free.

It can be tough to come out with the truth honestly about certain situations in your life. Especially when the truth can hurt the people you care about. For example, you and your wife may have separated for a short time, and during that, you slept with another woman. Now you and your wife have decided to come back together, but your mistress advises that she is three months pregnant. You have a tough decision to make here. Do you become a dead-beat father and avoid responsibility? Or should you be honest with your wife and risk the possibility of losing her?

The second option is the toughest, but it is the correct option. You must take responsibility for every decision you make in your life. Granted, you guys were separated at the time, but the result of your action is life-changing. You must make the decision, to be honest with her at all times and in all circumstances and tell her the complete truth.

The truth will hurt her, and there can be a high risk that you may lose her, but in the long run, she will respect and appreciate your honesty. You are a leader even in the darkest moments of your life. Even when you are in the wrong, you still are the leader.

In ancient times, leaders of war made the wrong decisions, and thousands of their soldiers were murdered. The bad decision by the leader did not make them any less of a man or a leader. They instead grew in knowledge and ensured the same decision was never made again. Your bad choices don't define you; instead, they groom you and make you a better man. You must not seek perfection in your life but instead seek growth. You will always be flawed throughout your life. However, if you stay firm in honesty and integrity, it will pay you back eventually, and believe me, the fruit will be the sweetest.

Chapter 43

She Must Trust Every Part of You

A woman must be able to look at you and trust each part of you. She must trust that you are headed in the right direction and can escort her along with you whenever needed.

Most women seem to want to be in control of everything in a relationship. However, they want to feel that they can be led by you too. She will not trust you if you aren't walking the universe in dominance and leaving your print. If you want your woman to trust you and reject the need to be in control, you must take control and steer your ship.

Now, do not misunderstand this. This isn't a call to boss her around or disrespect her, but a reminder to know where you are going spiritually, mentally, and financially. You must know how you will get there and ensure that you clear the road for her to follow you instead of her making her own way. If you appear uneasy or uncertain about the direction you are headed in, your woman will know it.

You don't have to be the wealthiest man or own ten businesses, but you must be wise in allocating your funds. You must not confuse these two, but instead, be sure where you are headed. Prove to her that your masculine core can be trusted and that she can rely on you in all ways. This allows your woman to remain calm with you because she knows where your values lie.

You must ensure that you are directing the relationship as well. You must confirm your morals and values are the same. Be the spiritual leader of your relationship. If your woman views you as a man that lacks confidence and leadership, she will attempt to lead herself. If every month the lights cut off because you would rather spend money at the casino instead of paying the bill, she will not be able to be calm in your presence.

Eventually, she will start to make decisions (which is the man's role), and you will begin to see the relationship go downhill. The gentleness she once had when speaking to you will cease. As she continues to be the leader, the relationship will fall apart, and the relationship will be guided by emotion versus clarity.

You must know your purpose and be financially in tune for your woman to remain calm while she is with you. To remain calm, she must look at you with extreme trust and know that you will guide her to the promised land. She must feel your deep love and trust your core instinct. As long as you are in control spiritually and financially and prove to her you are clear on your intentions, she will remain calm in her female nature and let you lead her.

Chapter 44

Dealing with Pain

As difficult as it may be, you must remove the outside opinions of being hurt and isolate yourself and go through every emotion of the pain. Because every moment you spend wallowing in your misery makes you stronger.

In the summer of 2020, I was in my career and preparing to purchase my first home. At the time, I was engaged to a woman with whom I had a lot of ups and downs, and truthfully, I played a role in the separation as well. However, I always tried to be the best man I could be and love unconditionally.

As summer continued, the relationship just became unrepairable, and we separated. A week later, I received notification that I was approved for my dream house. The house had four bedrooms, three bathrooms, RV parking, and a swimming pool. What kid didn't want a swimming pool growing up? I remember my best friend and my family being extremely happy.

As much as I wanted to be happy, I just couldn't fathom living in this home alone, knowing that I only purchased this with her in mind. I moved into my new home, and my first night there alone, I cried myself to sleep. I had no interest in anything, and I recall praying to God and begging the pain to be removed.

There and then, I made the decision not to lay with another woman or to turn to alcohol, but instead to feel the pain completely and not run from it. I began weekly therapy and expressed my emotions and concerns. I started reading daily and applying what I read throughout my day. Just as I felt myself improving, my grandfather passed away from COVID-19.

Here I am twenty-six years old, and I have everything a man could ever ask for, but deep down, I was broken. The only peace in my life was going to work as a police officer. I found more peace in responding to a shooting or homicide than I could in my own heart. One day, I made the decision to take control of my life and my hurt. For some reason, the pain of loss seems to impact us more at night. Ironically, my shift was throughout the night, and if I wasn't responding to a call, my brain was spinning.

On one evening at work, I observed a homeless male, and he appeared to be distraught and lost. The irony is, when I looked at him, I saw myself. I saw a man that was attempting to find his way, but he was running in circles. I rolled down the window to my patrol car, and I asked him if he had eaten today, and he replied, "I haven't eaten in three days." I realized that the pain in my life was bearable at that moment and that things could always be worst. I drove to a nearby burger restaurant and bought him as much food as he could eat.

As he stood in front of me eating, he began crying, and he said, "I took care of everyone in my life, but when I needed love, nobody showed up. Thank you for caring about me." I hugged the man, walked to my patrol car, and began crying uncontrollably because I was looking in a mirror when I saw him.

That is when I realized that the true purpose in life is in the service of others. A man who can give when broken will always remain in God's good graces. Each time I felt sick to my stomach thinking about being hurt, I gave to others. Ironically, the more I gave to others, the more I healed.

Brother's, when you are hurt by those that you love, you must feel every emotion of the hurt and never jump to the next woman waiting to accept you. Rebound can only give you temporary satisfaction and pleasure. If you do not deal with your pain and hurt, you will only traumatize the next woman you decide to date. Take your time and ensure that your next woman is your best friend, therapist, teammate and that she understands you.

Chapter 45

Don't Blame Her

During pain in a relationship, we tend to blame the other party rather than accepting an equal role played. You cannot clap with one hand; you need two to tango.

We all have been in a relationship that we tried in every possible way to make work, but it was never enough. The time soon came when you two agreed it was best to break up. An immature boy will react by pointing the finger, posting subliminal messages on social media, or spreading negativity about this person. A man who is focused on working on himself will isolate himself and reflect on the role he played to better understand his shortcomings and not repeat them the next time around.

You cannot grow through experiences by blaming others and playing the victim. We tend to believe that the person who committed the most recent act of betrayal is at fault. You must think of a relationship as a football game. For example, if Tom Brady throws an interception during the last drive of the football game, which causes the Tampa Bay Buccaneers to lose, he will be the reason they lost the football game.

Commentators and fans never view the game in its totality and will take to social media to completely downplay Tom Brady's ability as a quarterback. The fans totally disregard the fact that there are ten other players on the field with Tom Brady and that there are other factors of the game he cannot control. However, since his mistake is the last, the loss will be on his shoulders.

Similarly, in relationships, we must ensure we are looking at all phases of a relationship and not just the recent error. It is common practice for women to leave a relationship and down talk their ex to others. This is not because she truly feels this way, but more of a way to not accept her role in the failure of the relationship.

If she can paint you as evil and as a bad person in her mind, then she can train herself into believing you are these things. She doesn't understand that her emotional freedom lies in accepting her role in the failed relationship and in forgiving you for your shortcomings.

You must keep in mind that women reside in an emotional state, and when they have feelings of hurt or negativity regarding you, they will continue to stay in that state. You cannot focus on her reaction to the breakup or the rumors she is spreading. Instead, you must show humility and accept the role you played, and if possible, you should apologize to her. When you apologize, don't use words such as 'that is my bad' or 'my fault.' You must say, "I apologize for what I've done to you," or "I am sorry."

As you express these emotions of humility to her, you will be set free from the chains of animosity and bitterness. This will open doors for you to deal with your pain and be ready for the woman of your dreams, and you will be able to love her freely.

Chapter 46

Grow Through It

If a man does not embrace the opportunity or learn the lessons conflict brings, he is as good as dead. He may as well surrender his shield and yield.

When we are hurt, it breaks us to the core and leaves us feeling a sense of worthlessness. There is beauty in feeling these emotions, but the problem is when we reside in these emotions. You must feel the pain and accept the hurt, but never allow it to consume you. Specifically, with the loss of losing a person you care about deeply. If you make the decision to reside in anger, there is no way you can move forward.

The woman for you will always be optimistic about the potential of you. I am not saying that you can mistreat a woman and be unproductive but still receive the benefits of a productive man. I am just trying to give you the perspective and bring light to the saying, "what is meant for you, will be for you." It sounds cliché, and truthfully, you don't want to hear anything other than her voice during the pain.

It would be best if you did not force yourself into the life of anyone. When you are calling her phone a thousand times, and she is not answering, you are losing time that could be invested in bettering yourself and gaining some perspective. In a man's mind, you are showing her your commitment and obsession with her, but in her mind, you are insane. When she leaves you, nothing about you is attractive, and truthfully and as bitter as it may sound, she has probably already moved on.

Rather than basing your life on her, find the things that make you smile and force you to grow. Use this pain to motivate you and drive you to be the best man you can be. What good will you be to the woman who is heaven sent if you are obsessing over a person who doesn't want you? It is difficult, but if something isn't giving to you, it is hindering you. You must look at all things in your life and brain as one.

We will look at love differently than we look at a job because we only care about one of the two. However, it doesn't matter if your emotions are tied to a situation or not; if it isn't bringing you peace or adding to your life, it must go. You must love the person who loves you. No matter how many times you attempt to force a triangular-shaped object into an oval object, it will not fit. The only way it will fit is by breaking something. You don't need to be broken to pay close attention to things or a person in your life who no longer serves you.

As you sit in solitary, that is when you must genuinely dig deep and hold yourself accountable for your fault. You must sincerely apologize to her and return to isolation. You will go through every emotion, but the benefit of being unattended is that you will fall in love with yourself again. You don't realize it, but when you are in a relationship that isn't serving, you lose a sense of self-worth. You lose your individuality, and your focus becomes to make her happy rather than yourself happy.

Once you gain that love of self, you will begin to set boundaries for yourself, and they will soon become a part of you and your belief system. Without isolation, you will not be able to find yourself. Consequently, you will walk around like a wounded deer, just waiting to die.

Chapter 47

Playoffs

Life is a beautiful excursion that sometimes has turbulence, but in the end, the journey is gracious.

The pain makes the journey beautiful and worthwhile. How could we ever grow or educate others if we don't have the experiences to pull from? Look at life with a sense of optimism, and you will find understanding. You've come so far in this journey and will continue to gain knowledge. You've been preparing this entire journey for a quantum leap and now have it. You've prepared for it, and you knew things would manifest themselves as you continued to work. You have written down your goals and dreams after overcoming your trials, and now that they have occurred, you are in disbelief.

It should be no surprise to you that as you have followed the guidance of this book, many doors have opened for you. You are unique and one of a kind. You have already seen the bottom of the ocean, and the only way is up. There shouldn't be any more fear that you cannot withstand in your heart.

You are understanding that your experiences are only here as a guide or simply a reminder that you are gifted and chosen. You have come so far in this journey and are one step closer to being considered with all of the greats who have overcome difficulties. Persistence is all it takes, brothers. You must not ever give up. When you look in the mirror, say, "I am mighty, everything I want, I will have." The only thing stopping you is you.

The good thing for you is that you speak positivity into your life and will never stop yourself. You have now won the playoff game, brother. You have one game left. How do you want to be remembered? As a champion or a person who was never able to get over the hump in life?

Chapter 48

Championship

The pain of disappointment is haunting, but the joy of overcoming is the true definition of peace.

You have now overcome the pain and sorrow of your losses. Now it is about you and what makes you happy. Your life is no longer about the pleasure of others. You have taken control of your life and the things you allow to consume you. People around you are noticing your glow, and they are all inquiring about the smile you have. This is alarming to them because you were in a dark place a few months ago. They don't know that you have put in the work and have been patient with the process.

You are a leader, and truthfully, it isn't any of your business what they say. When you went into isolation, it was thought that you had given up and that life had defeated you. Instead, you went to the drawing board, opened your heart, and studied it carefully and thoroughly.

You missed out on outings with friends and deleted all of your social media. Nobody heard from you. It was like you disappeared and fell from the face of the earth.

Nevertheless, you were more focused on the process than the outcome and realized this too shall pass. You have now organized your life. The universe/God, your health, and your purpose are your priorities. You made yourself the best option, and you no longer tolerate disrespect from people or being treated as a second option. You now see that true happiness comes in serving the world with your gifts.

You have a different outlook on pain. Without a doubt, it was once fear and untreated trauma, but now it is seen as a blessing that you smile at unannounced. You have begun to love the people who love you and have vowed never to ambush your way into someone's life.

You now dictate the people whom you surround yourself with. You have set boundaries that all must respect, regardless of the duration of the relationship. You have removed yourself from negativity and live in a reality that you have created.

As you have progressed and have been staying focused, you have finally come to terms with the failed relationships of your life. You have accepted your role and have learned from your mistakes. You have vowed not to point the finger at others but to look at the man in the mirror. You have turned pain into passion and are now balanced from head to toe. Wherever you walk, your dominance is seen, and you are respected as the king you are. Throughout this entire journey we have been on together, you have been searching for one thing that is now found, YOUR CROWN.

Welcome home, KING!

Made in the USA
Columbia, SC
14 June 2022